Life *in the* Passenger Seat

Only God can turn a mess into a message & a test into a testimony!

Best wishes!
Stephanie

Life *in the* Passenger Seat

STEPHANIE DULIN

TATE PUBLISHING
AND ENTERPRISES, LLC

Life In The Passenger Seat
Copyright © 2013 by Stephanie Dulin. All rights reserved.

No part of this publication may be reproduced, stored in a retrieval system or transmitted in any way by any means, electronic, mechanical, photocopy, recording or otherwise without the prior permission of the author except as provided by USA copyright law.

All scripture quotations, unless otherwise indicated, are taken from the Holy Bible, New International Version®, NIV®. Copyright ©1973, 1978, 1984 by Biblica, Inc.™ Used by permission of Zondervan. All rights reserved worldwide. www.zondervan.com

The opinions expressed by the author are not necessarily those of Tate Publishing, LLC.

Published by Tate Publishing & Enterprises, LLC
127 E. Trade Center Terrace | Mustang, Oklahoma 73064 USA
1.888.361.9473 | www.tatepublishing.com

Tate Publishing is committed to excellence in the publishing industry. The company reflects the philosophy established by the founders, based on Psalm 68:11,
"The Lord gave the word and great was the company of those who published it."

Book design copyright © 2013 by Tate Publishing, LLC. All rights reserved.
Cover design by Rodrigo Adolfo
Interior design by Mary Jean Archival
Cover photo by Janie Jones
Back cover photo by Tara Vickers

Published in the United States of America

ISBN: 978-1-62902-832-3
1. Religion / Christian Life / Devotional
2. Self-Help / Personal Growth / General
13.11.21

To Jeremy—
Thank you for sharing the passenger seat
with me on this journey we call life.
I love you.

Contents

Introduction	9
Reflections on Turbulence	13
Reflections on Singleness	17
Reflections on Patience	21
Reflections on Heritage	27
Reflections on Persistence	33
Reflections on Sight	39
Reflections on Anxiety	43
Reflections on Faithfulness	47
Reflections on Bitterness	53
Reflections on Change	57
Reflections on Fear	63
Reflections on Forgiveness	67
Reflections on Discipline	71
Reflections on Interruptions	77
Reflections on Self-Esteem	83
Reflections on Love	89
Reflections on Second Chances	93
Reflections on Eternity	99
A Note From The Author	105

Introduction

"Be joyful in hope, patient in affliction, faithful in prayer." ***Romans 12:12***

I am a thirty-something, Christian, goody-goody girlie who is thrilled to have my twenties behind me. I am far from supermodel height and I am usually behind on the latest fashions, but I pride myself on having my daddy's blue eyes and sense of direction. I have had many curve balls thrown at me in my life and several have hit me straight in the head, but through it all, God has proven his faithfulness time and time again. I have learned that you cannot put God in a box, and that He is much more interested in our character than in our comfort.

When I turned the big 3-0, I began to look back on how my life had been spent up to that point. What mistakes had I made? How had I changed over the years? What was my passion in life? How did I want to spend my next thirty years?

(Did anyone else have a Tim McGraw song go through their head?)! All of these thoughts flooded my mind and what you are reading is a compilation of experiences from primarily my twenties and particularly from a certain unexpected life-changing event. I didn't know it then, but looking back I can see God's hand woven through each and every season that I went through. I have come to believe that God can turn any bad into good and that there are lessons to be learned in everything that we experience here on this earth. And I have learned that God knows exactly what we need even when we are so sure of what we want.

This is written to encourage that young person who cannot see past their Starbucks addiction and late night study sessions. This is written for the mature person who thinks that their life is over and feels like there is nothing more to live for. This is written to exclaim that our God is a BIG God and He is bigger than anything that we may face in this lifetime. This is written for my children in hopes that they will learn from my own personal setbacks and experiences. This is written for me, to appreciate what I have been through and to remind me of the power of forgiveness and His grace, and to hopefully avoid the same mistakes in my next thirty plus years. And, this is written for all of my friends and family to express my sincere gratitude for their unconditional love and support in my life.

Life In The Passenger Seat

What do you do
when your dreams seem to fade,
when the sky turns from blue
to a deep shade of gray.
It is easy to become bitter
as disappointments come to light,
two people who vowed to be one
contending who is wrong and who is right.
Emotions are hard to deal with
and the wound stings so bad,
as you deal with adjusting
to hopes that you once had.
But the heart has a way of healing
as you live one day at a time,
laughing becomes much easier
and words come out a little more kind.
We cannot go back and change
regrets and hurts from our past,
but we can learn a lot about ourselves
and can pray for a new love that will last.
I am blessed with friends and family
who showed their support to me,
and a loving God up in heaven
for his faithfulness, grace, and mercy.
Who knows what the future holds
in this year or another five
but 'for better or for worse'
I am truly thankful for my life.

—Stephanie Dulin

Reflections on Turbulence

> "Do not be anxious about anything, but in everything, by prayer and petition, with thanksgiving, present your requests to God. And the peace of God, which transcends all understanding, will guard your hearts and minds in Christ Jesus." ***Philippians 4:6-7***

In my grandparent's day in age, flying was for the privileged and the filthy rich. Now, with modern technology and the current invention of e-tickets anyone can book a flight for a decent price wherever they would like to go. You may not be able to fly to Yemen on Southwest, but there is definitely some airline that is willing to take you there.

My first experience with flying was when I was around 12 years old. My family and I flew from St. Louis to Indianapolis for a convention my parents had to attend. I was filled with nervous energy and excitement. I had no idea what to expect as I boarded the aircraft and stepped inside the cabin. After playing "rock, paper, scissors" for a window seat, I delightfully and humbly accepted the win and vowed that my brother could lean over me to sneak a peek.

I admit that science wasn't my forte and when the lesson of aerodynamics, gravity and wingspan were presented, more than likely I was sitting at my desk writing a note to a friend. The design of a huge metal tube catapulting through the sky at 30,000 feet above the earth doesn't make a whole lot of sense to me, but, at the time, that wasn't what my mind was focused on. My mom handed me some gum to start chewing before take-off and I sat back in anticipation at what was about to take place. We took our place in line on the runway and after quite awhile of taxiing, I wondered if it would just be quicker to *drive* the plane to Indianapolis.

In an instant we heard the sounds of the engine gearing up and in seconds we were lifting off of the ground. Everything on the ground got smaller and smaller as my eyes grew bigger and bigger. I was in awe as we made our way through a clearing in the clouds and the earth vanished. It was as if we had flown into heaven as we nestled on top of a never-ending blanket of clouds. The sun was shining on the horizon and the whole world seemed at peace. A drink of our choice, a free roasted peanut packet, an amazing view and everything was perfect. That was until we hit…turbulence.

My perfect experience of flying was shattered. I thought for sure that the mere jiggle of the plane meant that we were going down. I shot my mom a very concerned look but she didn't seem to notice as she sat there resting her eyes. "*How could she possibly sleep through this?"* I thought. The jiggle smoothed out and I thought that it was over. After the third time of this happening though, I couldn't help but wake my mom up to express my grief and of course, to tell her how much that I loved her just in case we weren't going to make it. But, to my surprise, she wasn't shaken at all. Instead she comforted me with the fact that this was a normal attribute to any flight and it had a name. Turbulence.

Normal or not, I didn't like it. I wanted to be on the ground, kissing it. For some odd reason, however, no one around me seemed affected by this sudden realization that we could be at death's door. The stewardesses kept answering call buttons, picking up trash and responding to the same question, "How much longer do we have?" In a strange sense, I was put at ease as I watched everyone around me and realized that no one else was fretting. I felt a calm come over me knowing that we were all in this together.

Life is a lot like flying. We are all in this life together even though we each have different destinations. Some experience the more luxurious seats in first class, while others risk getting their elbows knocked off by the food and drink cart. Some passengers get extra leg room, yet others are so cramped up in a position that they cannot feel their legs for days. Yet, no matter where you are sitting in the plane, everyone is vulnerable to turbulence. It happens to all of us. It is easy to whine and complain about life's turbulence, but it doesn't change the situation. Most of the time, you just have to ride it out, trust in the pilots, and hope for the best.

I will admit that I still get a little shaken up when I am flying and we hit turbulence. That 'fasten seat belt' comes on and I grip the seat, my book, or whoever I am flying with. It is in that time of uneasiness that I say a little prayer and I breathe in and out deeply. It is then, and only then, that I feel peace in the troubling situation. That no matter what happens, or how turbulent things get, things are going to be okay (even if it doesn't feel like it in the current moment). God never said that this life was going to be easy. A lot of people assume that Christians don't face a lot of turbulence, and if they do, that means that they are doing something wrong. But the truth of the matter is that God never promised us happiness in this life. He promises us "peace which transcends all understanding." This is the 'hard to fathom' peace. This is that true inner peace that only God can pour on us in the most difficult situations when we call on Him and trust that He is always in control.

Side view mirror: Are you experiencing any turbulence in your life right now? Take time and pray for God's peace which transcends all understanding. Pray for comfort and guidance in the situation. And, thank Him for what He is going to show you in the midst of your turbulence.

Reflections on Singleness

*"And we know that in all things God works for the good of those who love him, who have been called according to his purpose." **Romans 8:28***

Twelve years ago I knew what the plan for my life was. I was newly married and I had children on my mind. The way was paved. Or, so I thought. One night and one confession and my dream had ended. There was a Dead End sign on the road that I had been traveling on. I felt betrayed, angry, bitter, hurt, and completely broken, and I have to say, it was the best thing that could have ever happened to me.

Yes, you read that last line right. Sounds kind of crazy doesn't it? How could such a painful, unfair, and unexpected situation actually be considered a good thing? The thing is, at the time, it didn't feel that way, but since then, God has shed so much light over the circumstance that I cannot deny the fact that He was there through it all. During these times we ask ourselves the age-old question of "Why do bad things happen to good people?" Frankly, there isn't a "one-size-fits-all" answer to this one, but in my case I can answer by saying that it has taught me so much about life, love, and most importantly, my relationship with God.

Like I stated previously, I KNEW what the plan was for MY life. The problem with that I never really sought what GOD's plan for my life was. I tried to make it the way I wanted it to be. I had been a Christian since I was 12 years old and thought that I had wholeheartedly trusted God, but it turned out, I had entrusted nothing to him. Without even knowing it, I had asked God to take a seat next to me and had decided to drive myself. And let me tell you, it has been a hard lesson to learn.

Over the years after my divorce I struggled so much with being single. I grew bitter and angry as I saw all of my friends starting families of their own and I was starting completely over. Over and over I expressed my disappointment to God. Ok, honestly, I expressed my disappointment AT God. I just didn't understand. Granted, this whole time, God is still sitting next to me in the passenger's seat. I was having major road rage as He just listened, and tightened His seatbelt.

I certainly do not want to bore you with details, so let me just hit the fast forward button for you at this point. As my heart started filling up with bitterness, anger, and envy through this whole period, I made a lot of stupid, hurtful, and selfish mistakes. I was not focused on God whatsoever and my actions became witness to that. I still thought that I could be in control of my life and still make MY dream happen the way I wanted it to. After being consumed with pride and self-pity, I finally gave in to God as He had been whispering, "Please trust me. Hand over the wheel because you have had us lost for quite awhile now and I don't need to stop and ask for directions."

So, finally, I moved over to the passenger's seat. This whole time I had been so upset at the fact that I was single. My attitude was that being single downright stinks. Yet, oddly enough, when I was in the driver's seat, the only thing that I was driving towards was that unrealized dream. I was narrow-minded and focused on the wrong things. I had tunnel vision and I could see nothing around me. But, in the passenger's seat, I saw the open road. I saw the beauty around me, and the little miracles that God had been trying to show me the whole time. And, it was here that I became satisfied with being single. Because it was while I was single that I was able to truly focus on God and my relationship with Him. He wants us to find our joy in HIM. Not in anyone or anything else in this lifetime. He wants a deep relationship with us and He wants us to be in love with HIM and to know HIM more. All of a sudden being single wasn't so bad. My bitterness and anger slowly started to dissolve and I was able to rest in the arms of Jesus knowing that He had everything under control. Knowing He had an even bigger and better plan for my life than I could ever dream up myself. All I needed was Him. Being single didn't have to stink…it could be truly satisfying.

I started looking at my time of being single as preparation. He was preparing me for HIS plans and to be absolutely ready emotionally and spiritually for the man of my dreams, if that was what He had for me of course. Soon after my divorce I had thought that I had been ready to move on, but I was trying to find my joy in things of this world and looking back on everything now, I had so much to learn about myself. And, I learned that things become so much clearer when we see things on a different level and with a different attitude. A dear friend of mine once told me years ago, "A season of suffering is a small price to pay for a clear view of God." We may never truly understand why certain things happen in our lives and why things seem so unfair at times, but we can be reassured by God's promises in Romans 8:28. Without a doubt, making God the GPS of my life was one of the best decisions I ever made.

Side view Mirror: Are you struggling with where your life is at right now? Hand over the wheel and pray to God for clarity and direction. Rest in Him knowing that He is in control of your life, even if it doesn't seem that way right now. And, thank Him for the beautiful scenery that you are about to enjoy along the way.

Reflections on Patience

*"There is something worse than waiting on God. It is wishing that you had." **Anonymous***

I know how it feels to want something so bad that you don't care how you get it, you just want to embrace it as yours. I know what it is like to think "if I had '*xyz*', my life would be so much more complete and I would be a better person if only I could claim it as mine". I know what it is like to be impatient and to be ungrateful. And, I know what it is like to think that I am more knowing than God. I now know what a joke that is.

Years ago when I was going through my divorce I was bitter at a lot of circumstances and people. However, I thought that if I could just attain certain material possessions, my life would somehow magically get back on track and everything would just align itself in place. It all started with my car.

I highly disliked my car. Or, should I say, I highly disliked my ex-husband's car. Actually, in all honesty, I highly disliked my ex-husband so that is why I highly disliked my car because it is the car that I got in the divorce. There, the truth is out. So, there I am, with a decent car but I wanted something more. I wasn't looking at the fact that there was hardly anything left to pay on the car, it ran just fine, the gas mileage was great, I could afford the payments, and it always got me to point A to point B. Nope. I wanted my dream car. I wanted a SUV. I was single and hardly making ends meet but somehow I had rationalized myself into thinking that I was doing the right thing by purchasing another vehicle, my dream vehicle. If only my older self could go back and slap my younger self in the face.

I loved my SUV and I was on cloud nine. It felt great to drive around and show off MY car and be part of the SUV status quo. But then I had to make my first payment and my joy faltered. A payment that was double to what I had been making, and to a loan that was three times higher than the other car. But, still, I managed to rationalize it. Even as my debt increased (just so I could pay all of my monthly bills) I would tell myself that "it is a better car", "it is a safer car", "it will payoff in the long run", and "I made a great decision." Then gas prices sky-rocketed and on top of the monthly payment, car insurance, and gas, I finally came to terms with the fact that I bought the car because I wanted it, not because I needed it.

Unfortunately, that wasn't the only time that I had made a decision based on my wants. It took me awhile but I finally realized there was not a material possession that would bring me contentment and happiness and I had to change my thinking.

It has helped me to imagine life as a long road with many, many stoplights. It is so hard to wait and be patient. It never fails that when we have some place to be we end up hitting all of the red lights on our way there. We tend to focus our thoughts on what lies ahead and how we can get there in our record-breaking timing. We completely disregard the fact that the stoplight is flashing yellow or is a clear RED, and we zoom right through. Then we get in an accident and we are ticked off at the world. "This isn't fair!" "I don't have time for an accident!" "How did this happen, and WHY did this happen to ME?!" and the infamous statement, "This isn't *my* fault!" When, in all actuality, it is. If we would have been paying attention to the signs, there are certain predicaments, or accidents in this case, that we can avoid.

This analogy has been a vessel in my growth. If I don't take time to stop and be patient, I completely miss out on what is right in front of me. If I am not paying attention to everything else around me, I start to take things for granted. My friends, family, shelter, food, clothes, all of these basic necessities that I should have been thanking God for on a daily basis and didn't. Too many times I would be blessed with something and I wouldn't even know it because I was already looking for something more. Amazingly, once I slowed down and realized that what I have doesn't bring me happiness, I found true contentment and joy. I was less stressed and my anxiety wasn't as high. And, I was finally able to take responsibility for some of my past financial mistakes. It didn't mean that I didn't and wouldn't face any tough times, but I was finally able to appreciate everything that was around me and enjoy what I did have.

Steven Furtick, from Elevation Church, said, "Happiness is a symptom of circumstance, joy is a product of perspective." I absolutely love this statement because it helps me to understand the difference between happiness and joy. I have been challenged with many things on this journey called life and I now have to personally ask myself the following question when I would like to purchase something or do anything that involves money. "Will I survive without it?" I don't want to make my decisions on whether it will make me happy or not because happiness is a temporary emotion of our flesh. Joy is inner peace and gratefulness even when the situation is difficult and things don't go our way. It is focusing on eternal things rather than external 'blings'.

We hear the statement, "You can't take it with you when you go" and we laugh as we think of the hearse with a U-Haul attached to the back. But, yet, that is how we sometimes live our lives. That is how I was living my life. With all of this being said, I am still learning and growing myself! I have had to wait at several stoplights for longer than I would like to, but looking back now, I thank God that I did. In all reality, it is much better to wait than to find yourself in a mess that could have been avoided.

Side view Mirror: Have you been in a recent 'life accident'? Maybe one that could have been avoided? Pray to God for patience and contentment. Pray that He will fill your heart with the joy that you have been seeking. And, thank Him for the red lights that you come to in your life.

Reflections on Heritage

"God grant me the serenity to accept the things that I cannot change, courage to change the things I can; and wisdom to know the difference." ***Serenity Prayer***

On the outside, my family was the perfect nuclear family. Complete with my mom, dad, my brother and I, and two pooches. We had a beautiful home, went to church every Sunday, and even sat down to family dinners on most nights. If it sounds too good to be true, it was. Behind our closed doors and masks, my family was falling apart. The walls of our house were lined with tension and at nights I would lie in my bed as I listened to my parents fighting. I couldn't always make out the actual conversations but the loud mumbling and bickering through the walls was enough to let me know that the words being exchanged were not friendly ones. I was in a constant state of uneasiness as I sat on the floor with my head rested against my bedroom door. Out of habit, I would not climb into bed until there was silence for at least ten minutes. Once it sounded as if they were sleeping, things were calm and it was only then that I would feel a sense of peace in this nerve-wrecking situation.

Time and time again I overheard the phrase, "I am staying in it for the kids." It was hard to decipher how I truly felt about that phrase as a teenager. On one hand, I wanted nothing more than my parents to be together and for us to be a family forever, but on the flip side I also wanted nothing more than the fighting to stop and for them to be happy. And, unfortunately, that would probably mean that they would have to be apart in order to accomplish that. I distinctively remember wondering what it would be like if they got divorced and married other people. I dreamt of having two new and fun stepparents in my life, other brothers and sisters, and getting double presents at Christmas. How great would that be?! I had the perfect blended family picture in my head.

My parents did end up getting divorced and my brother and I were emotionally pulled in two separate directions. I happened to be in college at the time, and my brother was still in the midst of the turmoil at home. I have experienced, and observed in other children, that divorce affects children differently at every age. I can only express what I went through, and without sharing intimate details of our family circumstance, anger found its root in my heart. In my teens, I thought that it would be fun to have two separate families for double the love and double the gifts. But, when my parents remarried in my early twenties, I was realizing that two separate families also meant double the parents and double the criticism. Everyone had their own story, perceptions, experiences, priorities, and opinions to bring to the table. Put it all together and for some reason it did not add up to the perfect and well-balanced Brady Brunch family.

All families have their own issues and I have learned that ultimately the past does affect the present. If the past is not dealt with, the cycle of feelings and behaviors continue and end up seeping into other areas of our life. Unfortunately, I took a lot of harbored feelings from my parents divorce into my own marriage and I had to later admit to that fault. Since I had never really tried to understand where my feelings were stemming from, I became a victim and did not take responsibility for how I was contributing in my own personal relationships. Over the course of my twenties, I had conflicts with friends, my then husband, both of my stepparents and even my own parents. Unfortunately, this is when denial was playing full court. I just didn't understand how everything always happened to me, until I realized that the main denominator of many of my battles was in fact, ME.

It was definitely a gradual growth for me to come to terms with my own attitude, actions, and responses. And, it was quite humbling to say the least. I came to acknowledge that we inherit emotions just like DNA. Acceptance was a big determining factor in my healing. The Webster's Dictionary defines acceptance as "acknowledging what is true." I cannot go back and change my parents past or my past, but I can name it, claim it, and move on. How I respond to the past will determine my future, and I cannot waste any more time in the cycle of harboring past anger. There is a point where it boils up and explodes. If it is not cleaned up, the wreckage will stay around and everyone else around you will feel the affects as well.

With all this being said, I have to make it very clear by saying that even though my parents unfortunately did end their marriage, they were great parents to my brother and I. We had so many happy memories of our childhood and I will treasure those forever. Ultimately, as we grow up and mature, we are the ones responsible for our actions and our life. There are a lot of people who live in the past and have never dealt with particular issues. However, the only thing that we can do is to have unconditional love for them, hold onto God's truth, and pray. Pray for opportunities to grow closer to the ones that you may have kept out of your life because of pride or anger. Pray for past hurts and issues to be resolved within your family. And, pray that your loved ones will feel and know God as they learn to embrace each other again. It is not an easy road, but it is so much more fulfilling when you deal with patterns inflicted in your own life and give the past up to God.

I am happy to say that I have found healing and acceptance within many of my relationships with family members and friends. They are certainly not perfect by any means, but they are definitely a work in progress, which I am proud of. It was emotionally draining to take on everyone's hurts and it was a load off of my back when I accepted the fact that I did play a part in my own healing. It is not my job to change anyone's feelings or actions, nor does God even give us that capability to do so.

We all tend to wear masks at times. It is hard to show our real selves in fear of judgment, embarrassment, or ridicule. We all have families that are living in a society where 'abnormal' is defined as the new 'normal'. It is time to tear off the masks and redefine normality the way that God commands us when he said, "Love one another". He didn't add any exceptions, limitations, or conditions to this commandment. I am certainly not going to be naïve in thinking that we will get along with everyone who comes into our lives, but I have learned that when it is hard to love someone, including ourselves, it is much easier to lean on God for strength and pray for grace.

Side view Mirror: Are you experiencing turmoil within your family? Pray that God will provide you comfort and the right words to say in order to work towards healing. Pray that your family members will be open to new relationships and forgiving the past. And, thank God for the family members He gave you.

Reflections on Persistence

> "Does he not leave the ninety-nine in the open country and go after the lost sheep until he finds it? And when he finds it, he joyfully puts it on his shoulders and goes home." ***Luke 15:4-6***

He was an adorable little dog. A little fur-ball with the sweetest eyes and perfect face markings. Yet, in a heartbeat, he would become mean. Frightfully mean. A true Jekyll and Hyde story in dog-form. There were many occasions when I actually feared the little guy and wondered why he was in my life.

It was a cold January day in Kansas City. I had invited some girlfriends over for brunch and to see the quaint little house that I had just started renting during my pending divorce. I was already settling in, but it was quite the adjustment going from being married to living on my own again. Thankfully I had my big chocolate lab, Maverick, to keep me company, but after awhile I began to wonder who was going to keep Maverick company during my long days at work. Now that it was just the two of us, he would be home alone all day without anyone else coming in and out. I flirted with the idea of getting another dog, but quickly brushed it off every time the thought would enter my mind. I knew that I could not afford two dogs, yet every time I looked into Maverick's eyes, I could not help resist keeping my own eyes open for a perfect daily play mate and companion.

My best friend, Rachel, came over that day for brunch and brought along her dog, Callie. We joked that Callie had become Maverick's 'girlfriend' and we got them together any chance that we could. Rachel knew I had been contemplating getting another little pooch, and Callie was the perfect temporary fix when I thought Maverick needed a doggie-friend to play with. Girlfriends shuffled in and we began our chit-chats over home-made munchies. I was hanging out in the kitchen putting together another plate of yummies when I heard the barking.

Maverick and Callie were going crazy but I could not see any reason for their chaos from my window view. It wasn't until one of my friends said, "Look, over there!" that the stray dog caught my attention. He was roaming back and forth peering into the yard looking completely oblivious to why these two big dogs would be barking. I wasn't sure what to do, I didn't know anyone on my street yet but figured he was a neighbor's dog and he would just head on home in due time.

Soon I was distracted with another arrival and I was back in the party-mode.

Three hours later, my friends were putting on their coats to head out into the brisk snowy afternoon. As soon as the first guest opened the door to exit, low and behold, the stray dog walked into my house! I ushered him out into the backyard to hang with the other 'kids' while I said good-bye to the remaining guests. Maverick and Callie's sniffers were working full-time as the little guy stepped onto the back porch. They weren't quite sure what to think and I wasn't sure either. I knew that if Maverick had been lost and found, I would want that person to do anything they could to find me. Maverick was my 'baby', and the only family that I had in Kansas City. Looking at the little dog's ratted fur, it was obvious he had been wandering the streets for awhile, and I sympathized with his poor family. They definitely would be missing him. After feeding and bathing him, he perked up a bit and started exploring the house as Maverick watched in confusion.

The next morning I hung up "Found Dog" signs all over the neighborhood. There was one on every corner and at every stop sign. I thought for sure I would be receiving an exciting, heart-throbbing, sappy phone call from the family thanking me from the depths of their hearts for finding him. In the meantime, I named him "Graham" because his coat had a graham cracker coloring and "hey little guy" wasn't doing the trick in the command area.

After three weeks, I finally received a call, but it wasn't from the anxious family. It was from Animal Control stating they had seen my flyer and they knew whom the dog belonged to. Apparently they had caught 'Graham' several times wandering and the owners didn't seem to care much. And, come to find out, they lived only a block away from me, two street signs and two flyers away from my house. However, the man on the other line reported that he would be calling the owners to let them know the dog was with me. With this news, I began to wonder if I wanted to give him back. I was growing fond of the little guy. When I did receive that call from the rightful owners, I heard a demand to give the dog back instead of bottomless heartfelt thanks. We scheduled a time and I obliged. Maverick and Graham were still getting used to each other when Graham was given back. Again, Maverick just looked at me with more confusion.

Three weeks later we were back into our daily routine and I began preparing for a much-needed vacation to Florida to visit my brother. Two days before I was supposed to leave, I was pulling into my driveway and caught a glimpse of some familiar fur. It was Graham, in my fenced-in, locked-up backyard! Stopping the car and opening the door on autopilot I began talking to myself and trying to make sense of what was going on. That is when I saw the note. It read, "We do not want him anymore. He seemed happier here. He is yours." Standing in disbelief, I opened the gate to greet my new dog. But, he didn't seem happy. I could see the look of hurt, anger and rejection in his eyes. And, on the other side there was Maverick who just stood there looking at me as if to say, "Seriously, is he coming, going, or staying? What's the deal here?!"

Graham had just been dropped in my yard by his 'family' and he knew it. He looked so lost, sad and helpless. I tried to love on him but he wanted nothing to do with it. He began getting aggressive with Maverick, took off running when there was an open door, and snipped at anyone who tried to rescue him. Graham escaped on numerous occasions and my heart raced every time he took off. I would chase after him in hopes of catching him and bringing him home. The run and chase scenario became ritualistic and several times I broke down crying in the middle of the street. I was feeding and taking care of him, why didn't he realize how much I loved him and just wanted him home? Maybe he was afraid to let me love him in fear of being hurt again. Nonetheless, his defenses were up and he was a fighter.

I was torn. I knew I did not want any harm to come to Maverick or I, but there was something inside me that would not allow me to give up on him. I didn't want to be the next person to drop him somewhere. My vet was so patient and kind and understood my torn feelings in the situation. As funny as it sounds, he prescribed Graham some anti-depressants and encouraged me to try different reactions when he would act out. Eventually, and thankfully, Graham began to calm down and felt more at "home" with Maverick and I. It took quite awhile but I am happy to report that he became such a different dog. He was sweet, lovable, and had the best little doggie personality in the world. I am so glad that I did not give up on him and I could not have imagined life without him. When he passed away several years later I knew there would never be another Graham.

Have you been hurt? Have you been dropped by someone that you loved? Have you be wandering around this life feeling lost? God will rescue and go after anyone who runs away and fights against Him. He loves us unconditionally and will do anything He can to bring us back home. He rejoices when we run into his arms no matter what we have done, how far we have strayed, or how long we have been gone. God is always there, it is us that choose to be apart from Him. He feeds us, cares for us, loves us and yet we still seem to put up a battle in hopes to escape and live life on our own. I have learned that God's love is unconditional no matter what may happen and that He will never give up on me. In the words of Corrie ten Boom, "Yesterday He helped me, today he did the same. How long will this continue? Forever! Praise His name!"

Side view Mirror: Have you ever had any 'Graham tendencies'? Do you have a guard up in fear of being hurt again? Pray that you will feel God's arms around you. Pray for his overwhelming peace and presence to surround you. And, thank Him for always running after you.

Reflections on Sight

"We live by faith, not by sight." *2 Corinthians 5:7*

I was scared to death. Over the course of a few months, there had been something forming on the corner of my eye. In layman's terms, the doctor described it as a small pimple on my cornea. If the area went untreated, it could become infected and cause potential sight issues. I already had contacts and the worst vision in the world, so the thought of something extreme happening to one of my eyes frightened me. On the other hand, surgery freaked me out too.

Weighing the pros and cons, I reluctantly scheduled surgery to remove the 'pimple'. Unfortunately, it was not something I could be put to sleep for, and the thought of the doctor having to scrape something off my eye made me nauseated. The doctor said it would be a quick procedure and gave me some eye drops to prepare for the surgery. I was panicked and ask my friends to start praying. I just wanted to get it over with.

The big day rolled around and my mom came into town to escort me to the office since I was told that I would not be able to drive after it was all said and done. She sat with me as I anxiously waited to be called in. I was taken back to the pre-operation room and I realized that I was the youngest patient in there. It must have been two for one cataract day or something!

The nurse came over and began administering numbing drops in my eye. After a moment she grabbed my chart and began looking over notes. A confused look came over her face and she stated, "Now, what are we doing again today?" I couldn't tell if she was talking to herself or to me, so I ran through the history of my eye 'pimple' and its removal. After looking into my eye again, she said, "Well, honey, I just don't see anything to remove." I had noticed that the pimple had looked a little smaller over the past couple of days, but I assumed that size didn't matter when it came to the importance of the procedure. My nervous anticipation was the only thing that I had been concentrated on.

I was practically blind without my contacts and the two numbing drops were already kicking in when the doctor came over to talk to me. He asked the nurse what was going on and then he took a closer look at my eye. "Well, I'll be," he said with curiosity, "it's practically gone." He looked back in the nurse's direction, "It looks like we can take this surgery off the books today."

I thought that I had heard him wrong. "Seriously?! I don't have to have surgery? I can go?!" My heart leapt with joy and I nearly jumped out of the pre-op chair. The nurse laughed, the doctor smiled, and the senior citizen's bingo club looked over my way in wonderment. My excitement made an entrance into the waiting room before I did and tears of joy welled up in my eyes when I saw my mom. She assumed that I was trying to escape and was ready to march me right back in when I proclaimed, "I don't have to have surgery!" I was full of emotions. Shock, gratefulness, and amazement all consumed me as we made our way down the elevator. When I got home, I had three messages from friends stating they had been praying for me because they knew how worried I had been.

Several times God has used my sight to teach me lessons. I have lost many contacts over the course of twenty years and have found them in some unusual ways only after I would calm down, take a breath, and ask God to help me in my search. God knows how much I rely on my sight and how important it is to me. Sometimes things are taken away from us to teach us needed lessons but other times he simply asks for something just to see if we are willing to trust Him with it. I do believe that God had his hand on me as I went in for surgery that morning. And, I do believe with all of my heart that He healed my eye.

Peter lost sight of God when he was asked to walk out into the water. God simply asked Peter to trust in Him and look towards Him. However, Peter got scared and looked away. It was then that he sank. We should always fix our eyes upon Jesus and look up to Him when we are scared. Don't look down at the situation at hand. We cannot get through it on our own. We need His help, His guidance, and His comfort. When we seek Him first and keep our eyes fixed upward we will begin to see and experience God's little miracles in our lives.

Side view Mirror: Have you taken your eyes off of Jesus? Pray for help in seeking Him daily. Pray for guidance and comfort. Fix your eyes upward and learn to trust Him. And, thank Him for the things he gives us and takes away.

Reflections on Anxiety

"An anxious heart weighs a man down, but a kind word cheers him up." ***Proverbs 12:25***

It was early in the morning and I had a long day ahead of me filled with clients, paperwork, meetings, and appointments. At the time I was working with adults who had mental disabilities and my first stop of the day was to pick up two ladies and escort them to day rehabilitation. I arrived at their house and everything was going according to plan. Staff had them dressed, they had been given their medications, and their lunches were packed. I helped them both to my car and with a little awkwardness and physical exertion, was able to get them both buckled up for safety. One of the ladies had a walker and I went to go put it in my trunk. Unfortunately, when I threw the walker in, I also accidentally dropped my car keys into the trunk as well. I realized this as the door fell shut and it was too late. Unfortunately, my sporty little car's back seat did not come down for me to reach through and get the keys. I had two clients sitting in my car, I had a schedule to stay on top of, and I found myself in a pickle. It wasn't Monday, but it sure felt like it! Instantly I began to panic.

Thankfully I had a work cell phone on me and immediately called one of my co-workers in a plea to come and save us. I knew that I had a spare car key in my office desk and my only thought was that I needed that key. My co-worker said that she could go get the key and bring it to me but that it might be awhile because she needed to take her children to daycare. However, before she took them to daycare, she still needed to feed and dress them, along with herself. Talk about a change of plans in the schedule, for all of us.

Almost an hour and a half later, my amazing grace showed up with the key. In the exchange, she laughed and said, "Man, you need to get a car with a trunk release button in it!" My eyes darted to the floorboard of the driver's side, and sure enough, as plain as day, was a button with the trunk release symbol etched on top. My hour and a half long dilemma could have been solved in 10 seconds. Once my co-worker saw the embarrassment distort my face, I knew this would be a situation that I would never, ever, live down.

Now, I am totally cool with you rolling over in laughter, but before any of you visually write the word 'IDIOT' with a permanent marker across my forehead or make any hair color comments, hear me out. First of all, I had just purchased the car and my previous car had not had a trunk release button (seriously). I was not used to having this incredible feature and was oblivious to the fact that my new car had this lifesaver installed in it. Secondly, my reaction was made out of stress instead of common sense. Instead of thinking about a possible magical button, my thinking was narrow-minded and my only thoughts were, "I have no key, this is bad, I am in trouble." Even in the waiting period, I was thinking about my affected schedule and was attempting to salvage the soon-to-be missed meetings and appointments due to the fact that I thought I was unable to get around. I didn't look where I needed to.

Have you ever been so stressed that you ended up doing something embarrassing? If not, I suggest you stop reading this and look for your pulse! Unfortunately, stress and embarrassment happens to the very best of us. Without even thinking you put the milk in the cabinet instead of the refrigerator, you spray Lysol in your hair instead of using the hairspray, you wander into the wrong bathroom, or you put your shirt on backwards and head to work. These are the caution sign moments where we need to take a breather and slow down. Think things through before you freak out. Stop trying to do everything on your own. Calm yourself, focus, look up, and pray to God for a trunk release button.

Side view Mirror: Have you been stressed out lately? So stressed that you have ended up doing something embarrassing? Pray for patience and calmness. Pray for 'caution sign moments' and for clarity to see them. And, thank Him for the times when he shows you a 'trunk release button'.

Reflections on Faithfulness

"For great is his love toward us, and the faithfulness of the Lord endures forever." ***Psalm 117:2***

My quaint one and a half story house was perfect. The design was perfect, the yard was perfect, the size was perfect, and my rent was perfect. I had been renting this perfect house for almost two and a half years when the owners came to tell me they were selling it. My heart leapt with joy, *maybe I could buy it!* But, my joy quickly dissolved when they told me what they would have to sell it for. Without a doubt, it was by far out of my price range even if I wanted to buy a house. I was overcome with sadness. The house meant a lot to me. I had made it my home and I had hoped to one day call it my own. I was certain that I would not be able to find a better or more perfect place.

When reality struck that I would have to find another place to live, I felt a sense of depression and began flipping through the newspaper and browsing online. Rachel, my best friend and a realtor, handed me pages of possible houses to rent, but unfortunately, most of the houses that I looked at did not accept pets. That was a problem since I now had two dogs.

Out of curiosity, I thought that I would go ahead and look at houses to buy instead of rent. Buying a house definitely meant extra expenses and a possible increase from my monthly rent payment. I wasn't sure if I could swing it, but I didn't think it would hurt to look at the inexpensive houses that were out there. I suggested this new thought to Rachel and the next morning I had a list of ten houses in my inbox. Sure enough, as I scrolled down the list, the only ones that were in my price range were houses that were in a bad area or major fixer-uppers. My hope was fading fast until I saw it, the very last one on the list. It was the cutest little brick shack that I had ever seen and I let out a shrill, "Oh my goodness, that's it!" I rushed to the phone to call Rachel to set up a viewing.

Rachel had been a realtor for seven years at this point. She had sold many, many houses in the same area for years and knew each street, stop sign, and business. So, when I told her I had to see that particular house, you can understand why I was surprised when she responded with puzzlement. I reminded her of the list she had emailed me and told her it was the last one on the list, "You know the cutest little brick shack ever, number 1216?!" Much to my surprise, she told me that she was not sure what I was talking about but that she would look up some information and would get back to me.

I have been known to be a little crazy at times, but I knew what I had seen. I patiently waited for her call as I set my eyes on my computer screen and memorized the details of the house. Later that same day, I received my anticipated call. She had found the location and had arranged for a viewing the next afternoon. I was thrilled! As we drove over to the house that Sunday I tried to calm my excitement. I certainly did not want to get my hopes up, but I was finding it hard not to! After all, I had not even seen it yet, I had no idea if I would even be eligible for a house loan, and I knew buying a house was not a quick purchase that you could pick up in the Express lane at Wal-Mart.

My elation was unavoidable as soon as we stepped inside the front door. It definitely needed a little work and some paint but it was a perfect apartment-sized house for my 'boys' and I. It wasn't as big as the house that I was renting but that was okay with me, I could deal with the loss of space. My biggest question was, "What did the yard look like?" That was really important with having two dogs who needed their space to run. Rachel and I walked outside and my mouth dropped in awe. I was shocked. I could not believe what I was seeing. "Are you kidding me?!" was all that I was able to spit out. Rachel, too, was in obvious shock. It was like we had just opened the door to the promise land and Jesus himself was standing there with Ed McMahon and a million dollar check. With all exaggerated jokes aside, it was absolutely stunning. The yard was plush, green, and stretched out like a football field. There was a nice little patio with steps that led down into the beautiful grassy area, a chain linked fence to surround the property, a cute white shed with ivy and gorgeous red roses crawling up its side. And, in the back corner of the yard, was none other than a beautifully constructed wooden gazebo complete with flower boxes and lighting.

After many moments of taking in the captivating sight, I turned to Rachel and blurted out, "So, what do you think?" She was still canvassing the area but her amazed look did not have to offer any words. She answered by stating that she had been showing houses in this particular area and in this particular price range to a young couple for the past three months and this house had never appeared in her findings. The paperwork stated that it had been on the market for a month and if the young couple would have seen this house they would have, without a doubt, made an offer. This house by far exceeded anything she had shown them and we both stood there trying to make sense as to what was going on.

On my drive home I was overwhelmed with emotion. I knew that God's hand was on the situation and I could rest easy knowing He would take care of me. I knew that if He wanted me to buy this house He would make it possible. And, I knew that I could not force my own hand or change the situation. I didn't know what was going to happen next, what the process was, or what to expect, but in the weeks following He proved His faithfulness and everything fell right into place. The inspection went smoothly, the initial fees were covered by unexpected gifts, my loan went through, and I found myself signing my life away and being congratulated on becoming a home-owner only four weeks later. And, much to my surprise and excitement, my mortgage payment was only a $1.99 higher than what my monthly rent had been.

Too many times I have whined, complained and questioned God about what He was doing in my life. Didn't He know that my rental was perfect? Why did I have to move? Hello God?! Remember me?! I remember sitting in despair over the fact that I would not be able to own my 'perfect' rental house and wondering how God could bring anything better than what I already had. But, in all actuality, He saw the bigger picture and He did have something better for me. My narrow mind just couldn't see past what my eyes could see but He knew exactly what I needed. From that move I enjoyed living closer to my best friend, watched my dogs play in their nice big yard, made friends that I would not have met otherwise, and found greater independence in owning my own house. (I laughed at the irony of my new address as I was living in a town called Independence)! There was no doubt in my mind and heart that God had ordained these happenings and He had led me to the place He needed me to be. He is forever faithful to us even when we cannot see, understand, or explain the situation that we may find ourselves in. God sees the completed picture before a brush stroke is ever made. Let Him prove His faithfulness to you. It is so fun to see and experience what He has planned for us if we just let Him guide us.

Side view Mirror: Have you been whining to God about something that has not been going your way? Pray that you will see the path being paved for you. Pray for His will to be done, not yours. Be slow to anger and trust that He has everything taken care of already. And, thank Him for what He is about to do.

Reflections on Bitterness

"Do not give the devil a foothold." *Ephesians 4:27*

I had a secret. It was eating away at me and it was something I was in complete denial about. I went to bed with it, woke up with it, and took it to work with me. I put my outgoing personality and smile on my face on a daily basis so nobody knew what I was hiding. My secret was I was living with a horrible sin called Bitterness. You might not realize this is a sin, after all, there is not an eleventh commandment that says, "Thou shalt not be bitter", but the truth of the matter is that bitterness is a sin, one that damages us inside and out.

Bitterness was my rebound relationship after my divorce. It was a controlling and unhealthy relationship but I have to admit that it kept me company and I clung tightly to my new love. When I was lonely, it was there. I could count on it at any hour of the day, any hour of the night. It was there for me and we became inseparable. I knew it wasn't something

I should hang onto, but I felt as though I had a right to be in this relationship. However, in my attempt to keep it under wraps it unfortunately began to seep out and affect my work, attitude, faith, and even other relationships and friendships in my life.

I had been harboring this for a very long time. It had been hindering many aspects of my life and had become a barrier to my emotional healing. When God confronted me about this issue one weekend, I experienced a pendulum of emotions. On one hand, I was grateful for the wake-up call, but on the other hand, I knew breaking up was a very hard thing to do. Bitterness was a comforter and a contender. It was a friend and an enemy. It was a satisfying feeling but yet so unsatisfying. It was wrong but it felt so right. I wasn't sure how to say good-bye to this long-term relationship, but I knew that I had to. It was time.

If I would have had to sit in front of Dr. Phil many years ago he would have coined me as a 'right-fighter' and one who had several Emmy nominations to the victim roles I had been playing. I was in complete denial that my relationship with Bitterness had overtaken me to the point where I didn't even realize I was standing in a hole. A hole that I had dug for myself, and when I eventually looked up from my shoveling, there was not a whole lot of light left. My face was covered, my arms were tied, and my heart was in bondage. More than ever I knew I needed God's help in this mess. Even Houdini could not have gotten out of this one.

I broke up with Bitterness then and there. It was not easy, this had been a comforting and reassuring relationship for so long, but I knew that if I wanted to truly heal, I would have to let go of it completely. Bitterness did not take the news well and would show up often in attempt to win me back any time that it could. However, slowly, with God's help, I began to break free. I took ownership in my past mistakes and faults. I confronted people who I had hurt. I sought God's grace and mercy. I began to practice God's commandments and surrounded myself with fellow believers and encouragers. And, I came to terms with the fact that I had to truly 'die to self' if I wanted to experience the true freedom that only God could provide.

Words cannot express the freedom I found when I chose to release the bitterness that had overwhelmed my heart for so long. The stronghold was lifted and the burden was taken off of my shoulders and laid at the feet of God. I was free at last and it was so refreshing. My attitude, thoughts, words, and behaviors began to change. I knew that if I was to honor and glorify God, I could not look back and allow bitterness to consume me again. I am not saying that living without bitterness has been easy. In fact, it is something that I have to give up to the Lord everyday. However, I now realize the bondage I was in when I was trapped by bitterness and it is something that I never want to experience again. Thank God for the freedom we have in Christ Jesus if we are willing to relinquish our sins to him. I cannot change what happened in my past, I cannot change words that were exchanged or the hearts that were broken. I cannot change anyone else but myself and I am so grateful that I made the decision to come clean.

I have learned that bitterness is a terrorist and when we allow bitterness into our life we become vulnerable to Satan's agenda. Ephesians 4:27 states, "Do not give the devil a foothold." In other words, don't give Satan any reason to smile! His only intentions are to steal, kill and destroy. Anytime we allow someone else's words, actions, or behaviors to bring our pulse to a boiling point, remember who you are giving control to. More than likely, the people who have hurt you or made you outraged have already moved on and haven't even given you a second thought. However, those people will always have control over you if you never let it go. I am not suggesting that a person practice passivity, or become another one's doormat when confronted with tough life situations, but I do know from personal experience that when you let go of grudges, the world is a lot nicer of a place to live in. And, you make the world a nicer place too.

Side view mirror: Have you been in bondage due to bitterness? Pray that God will help you to break free from this captivity and that you will live the life that He has designed for you. Thank Him for His love and the gift of freedom.

Reflections on Change

> "Even though I walk through the valley of the shadow of death, I will fear no evil, for you are with me; your rod and your staff, they comfort me." ***Psalm 23:4***

I had lived in the Midwest all of my life. I had experienced the unpredictable weather conditions, including an October blizzard, a damaging ice storm, and many tornados (the main reason why basements are hot commodities for Midwest folk). I knew the sights and smells to the changing seasons and I knew how to prepare for such times. The Midwest embraced my family and friends and was my comfort zone. It was my biological home and the thought of moving away didn't cross my mind.

In the fall of 2005, I reached a breaking point in my life and the only thing that made sense for me was to move. Even though the Midwest was home to most of my friends and family, it had become a place where I had experienced hurt, pain, betrayal, and disappointment, and frankly, I was ready for a change. In a series of events, God paved the way for me to move and I soon found myself living in Arizona. I had visited the Phoenix area with my church youth group after my senior year in high school and one of the only things I had remembered about that particular trip was that we all came back with shirts that read, "I survived 121 degrees".

It was called a 'dry heat', and I was shocked at how much easier I breathed without humidity. The atmosphere and climate were completely different. Everything was brown, cacti replaced big leafy trees, and the yards looked like miniature putt-putt greens. It took me awhile to see it, but I began noticing that it was one of the most beautiful places I had ever been to. The mountains were breathtaking, the air was crisp, and the blue sky and sun were out on a daily basis. Some described Arizona as hell on earth due to the impressive high temperatures, but to me, it was heaven. Not only was it a wonderful place to physically live, it was here that I finally began to heal emotionally and spiritually.

When I moved, I was excited to start a new chapter in my life, but what I didn't realize was that God was taking me out of my Midwest-comfy-living for a reason. In the Midwest my vision had become clouded by my wants, needs and desires, and my relationship with God had started to suffer because of it all. He needed to take me out of my comfort zone and place me in a position where I only had Him to depend on. I knew a few people out in Arizona, but I did not have a

LIFE IN THE PASSENGER SEAT

church home or job established when I made the big cross-country move. I had to find my security in Him, and in that time of humility it allowed me to become vulnerable to His wants, needs and desires for me and my life. It was hard *not* to experience God living in Arizona. There was evidence of God's work in the majestic mountains, the blazing sun, and the clean atmosphere. I dove into a Christ-focused church and met some godly, spirit-filled people and made eternal friendships. It became very natural to seek God, feel His presence, and be in tune with what He was teaching me. I could not deny God's hand was on my life.

It wasn't long before the "Valley of the Sun" became my home and any chance I could get I would find a trailhead and hike up one of the local mountains. There were several mountains circling the Valley and I vowed that I would not take them for granted. I remember the first time I hiked up a mountain by myself, and the exhilaration I experienced when I reached the top and looked over the city. It was the most amazing view and if the sun hadn't started to set, I could have sat up there all day. I found solitude and felt at peace at the top of the mountain. Life was happening right below me but the world seemed to be moving in slow motion from my vantage point.

We all experience living in the valley at some point in our lives. We live in difficult times and the lows are often unbearable. God wants to meet us where we are but He also wants to lift us up, high on the mountaintops where we are in a position where it is impossible to deny his existence. He needs us to make time for Him and to seek Him. And, He desires for us to remember those mountaintop experiences when we find ourselves back in the valleys.

After only two years of living in Arizona, God made it very clear to me that I was to move to Florida. I was very sad and disheartened to leave my home in Arizona and found myself somewhat sad after living in Florida for only a short time. I began to realize that I was so focused on missing Arizona I wasn't even giving Florida a chance! However, in this time I was reminded that this earth is not our home. As Christians, we are aliens here and should feel uncomfortable if we are not in the presence of God. We may move all over the country but heaven will ultimately be our eternal destination and home. Without a doubt, it will be more beautiful than any place that we have ever seen in this world.

Sometimes God requires us to be taken out of our comfort zones in order to accomplish what He has planned. We may never know the reasons on this side of heaven why things happen or why He places us in different surroundings, but I have learned time and time again that God knows what He is doing and it is not for me to decide, discuss, rebel against or fight about. In my life, it is during those times when He has taken me out of my comfort zone that I have grown so much with Him. It is easy to get into our daily routines, lifestyles and rituals and leave God on the sidelines waiting for us to make time for Him. God does not want to be a convenient friend to us. He wants us to continue to grow in Him daily and to share His light with others.

I will be honest and say that because of the people I met, the lessons I learned, and the experiences that will forever be with me, I will always consider Arizona the 'Valley of the SON' and my home away from home. However, as much as I would love to live in Arizona again at some point, I really have no idea what His plans are for my family and I. But I am thankful for God guiding me to the desert in the time of my life where I needed Him most.

Side view mirror: What valleys have you been in? What mountains have you climbed? Pray that He will guide you through the valleys and bring you to the mountaintops. Pray that your experiences will be used for His glory. And, thank Him for His constant presence.

Reflections on Fear

> "So do not fear, for I am with you; do not be
> dismayed, for I am your God. I will strengthen you
> and help you; I will uphold you with my righteous
> right hand." *Isaiah 41:10*

My mom still tells the story to this day. I was four years old and I wanted to go to gymnastics class. She took me, I screamed and cried to go home, and that was the first and last time that I ever considered becoming a gymnast. No one had hurt me, no one had embarrassed me, and yet I was fearful of something that I had not even tried before. Unfortunately, I carried this handicap with me throughout much of my life. I didn't try many different foods, I struggled to expand my horizons, and I inhibited myself from at least trying certain skills in my younger years.

I remember watching my dad eat spinach for dinner with a grossed-out look across my face. He would catch my stare, make Popeye biceps with his arms, and with a big smile across his face he would exclaim, "Yummy!" I understood the correlation but his elation did not create a desire for me to try the green slimy stuff. I already had it in my mind that I didn't like it. And, how could I? Have you *seen* cooked spinach?

Let's look at the term *fear* in two separate ways. In the physical sense, fear can be debilitating, but in the spiritual sense, it can be rejuvenating. Fear in the physical sense leads us to limit what we may do and experience because we are scared. However, fear in the spiritual sense shows reverence to a God that is almighty and powerful beyond our comprehension. When we fear God, we are in awe of his majesty and who He is. We should not be scared to go to Him or have a relationship with Him. We should respect and be overwhelmed by the very thought that He loves us so much that He came to die for our sins. We may fear certain life experiences, but the fear that we should have toward God should not debilitate us, but should rejuvenate our spirits and our lives.

When I was 28, I finally experienced my first gymnastics class. I wasn't taking the class, I was actually leading it. Due to my growing passion for both kids and fitness, I began teaching children's fitness classes, which ironically involved many gymnastics skills and lessons. In my classes I began observing children who would cry and scream when we asked them to try something new. Without force, we would reassure the child that we would be with them and we would not let them fall. Reluctantly, and usually still with tears, we guided them through a gymnastic skill and helped them learn something new. Through the flips, their frowns would eventually turn upside down and on many, many occasions the child did not scream and cry to go home, they screamed and cried for "more".

God wants our fear to be used to bring us closer to Him. We should humble ourselves in His presence and position ourselves in a way that we live our lives fearing Him. Often, when we try something that we have never ventured out and tried before, we experience a thrill, a feeling of satisfaction. We cannot honestly be in fear of something if we have never even tried it before. How can you suggest the feeling of fear in something if you have never experienced it? How can you truly know God if you have never asked Him into your life? In our lives, if we fear something, we may never know how fun and satisfying it really could be. In turn, if we fear God, we will know and understand how fun and truly satisfying this life can be. It has taken me awhile but I have finally learned what it means to fear God. And, I am proud to say that I am now an avid spinach lover.

Side view mirror: Do you live in fear? Pray that God will ease your anxiety and will calm your fears. Pray that He will give you strength to step out of your comfort zone and that you will experience true joy. And, thank God for His power and might.

Reflections on Forgiveness

"Father, forgive them, for they do not know what they are doing." *Luke 23:34*

It was a Tuesday night when I found out. Reality kicked me in the face leaving my spirits black and blue. My assumptions were no longer something I had made up in my mind, but the hard reality that my two and a half year marriage was clothed in betrayal, distrust, and lies. It was true, my husband had been having an affair. A long-term one in fact. She was a fellow teacher, neighbor, and friend. I felt a new emotion for days, weeks, and the months that followed.

Oddly enough, one of the first emotions I felt was relief. I was relieved the truth was out, I was not actually crazy, and I could finally put one foot forward ever since those assumptions had gotten the best of me. Please hear me though. I am not condoning nor am I advocating for divorce when I share this feeling of relief with you. I didn't shout 'freedom' and have a party when my marriage fell apart. Instead I was reacting out of sheer physical and emotional exhaustion and a feeling of peace that only God could pour upon me.

In attempt to find courage and dignity through the ordeal I remember emailing my soon-to-be ex-husband soon after the affair surfaced stating that I had forgiven him. I thought by writing those words it meant I could soon move on and find happiness, instead of the hopeless feeling that had been consuming me for well over a year. However, the feeling of relief was only temporary and I realized that I hadn't actually forgiven him. They were just empty words from an attempted martyr heart.

I have written numerous times in these reflections about the anger and bitterness that overtook me. Even if I would have spoken, yelled or texted 'I forgive you' to my ex-husband a thousand times, I was never going to mean it in my heart because anger and bitterness had bound me from feeling that true emotion. I had always heard about the 'ultimate betrayal' and once I experienced it firsthand, I finally understood and realized the severity of the name. I was beginning to think that I would never be able to forgive him. And, heck, why should I?

During my time of questioning and whining, it was very easy for others to spout off the "forgive and forget" and "there are other fish in the sea" speeches. What people didn't realize was the fact that God does not always grant amnesia at our request, and yes, there may be other fish in the sea, but there are also sharks and piranhas swimming in that sea as well.

Forgiveness was far from my radar as I began building up a wall full of disappointing dates, unrealized dreams, and diminished hope. I was mad at my ex-husband for where I was in my life.

Poor me, poor me. Yet, I was the one holding myself captive and it wasn't until four years later that this revelation was realized. Once I clung onto that truth, I was finally able to give God those past hurts and emotions that had been weighing me down for so long. In its place I unexpectedly felt compassion. I didn't want the worst for my ex-husband, I didn't want to wish a Santa Claus belly and an early onset of male-pattern baldness on him, and I declined the thoughts of becoming a part of the Lorraina Bobbit fan club (case and point that bitterness does *not* come from God and is indeed a sin)! And I must say, this was quite an improvement in my scheme of thinking over the years, and clear evidence that I was making some progress in my healing.

One of the most humbling scriptures to read in the Bible is Luke 23:34 when Jesus is dying on the cross and he states, "Father, forgive them, for they do not know what they are doing." Think about it. Jesus is experiencing an incomprehensible, excruciating, and unfair death but yet He is expressing compassion and forgiveness to those who are killing Him. Little did the chief priests and soldiers know what God's plan really was as His Son hung there on that cross. He was dying for them. He was dying for *us*.

Jesus has forgiven me over and over in my life for sins I have committed. Who am I to be forgiven time and time again, but yet not offer it? Who was I to claim that I was a Christian but not forgive someone else? I had been so angry at what he had done, that I had totally disregarded any contribution or fault of my own in the dissolution of our marriage. I needed to forgive myself, and in doing so, it was much easier to forgive my ex-husband and to let the past be the past. I am not saying I have forgotten everything that happened, nor am I saying that my ex-husband's affair was justified by any means, but I certainly do not dwell on the past anymore. I like to use the phrase "forgive and be free". In doing that, I no longer rehash old memories and feelings, which has enabled me to move forward instead of being stuck standing with my feet in two concrete bricks. Forgiveness breaks the concrete bricks that we have poured in our lives and allows us to move more freely. Only through Him can we feel His grace and offer true forgiveness.

Ironically, the day I offered true, heartfelt forgiveness to my ex-husband in a new email, I was thrown the most unexpected, amazing, and memorable surprise birthday party of my life. And, I truly believe, it was a day full of rejoicing not only on earth, but in heaven as well.

Side view mirror: Are you struggling with forgiveness? Do you live with the notion that you have to 'forgive and *forget*'? Pray that God will give you the strength to offer forgiveness and will set you free. Pray for healing and hope. And, thank God for the cross.

Reflections on Discipline

"Train a child in the way he should go, and when he is old he will not turn from it." *Proverbs 22:6*

Our staff had nicknamed them the Evil Twins. They were not just in the terrible-two phase anymore, they were three year-old terrors. They would hit, kick, and spit on the teachers and other children during class. Where was their mother during this chaos you may wonder? Right next to them claiming that she did not believe in discipline. Now, I understand I have not been through the birthing process (my sons are adopted) but I do feel as if I have a lengthy resume of child development experiences and credentials, including being a mother myself. So I pray there will not be any parents who will hunt me down and criticize my thoughts and observations here.

I distinctively remember being a young child and sitting in church one Sunday morning focused only on a Strawberry

Shortcake coloring page. All of a sudden my mom shook my leg and whispered, "Listen to this." It was then that I heard the pastor preach, "Discipline is out of love. Parents who love their children discipline them." Since I was a child, I did not understand my parent's intentions when I got into trouble. But, that Sunday morning message slowly began to sink in through the years.

Discipline is not beating a child for getting out of line, it is taking the time to show them the difference between wrong and right. And, if it is not started at an early age, it will be harder to teach and follow through with as an adult. These early lessons carry on and will be evident in every aspect of our lives. I love the phrase, "It is easier to train a child than to fix an adult". Children are sponges and as I have mentioned in an earlier reflection, whatever happens in our past will influence our future and who we are. I have observed children who have parents who discipline and parents that do not. I am frequently sad, annoyed and frustrated when I am around those children who do not receive discipline at home. They are often out of control, disrespectful, and rarely obedient. I have learned that when it comes to parenting, children need three things; love, consistency, and discipline.

Before my own children came along, I had my two dogs. Remember my sweet little one, Graham? Since he had been a stray dog, he had already been influenced by former owners and anything else that he learned while he wandered the streets. I wasn't sure how old he was when I found him, but I could tell by his actions and reactions that he was treated poorly in his early years. And, it was I who ended up paying the consequences for his lack of discipline. I was at my wits end, and I admit, I had no idea how to solve the problem. Unfortunately, I could not go back and change how he had been treated in the past.

Thankfully, a couple of years after adopting Graham, I began dating a man who had some experience in dog training skills and he generously took the time to take the 'boys' under his wing. One day, as I was on my way home, he called me with a break-through. He started the conversation with, "Don't be mad". He went on to explain that while he was playing ball and giving personal attention to Maverick, Grahamy expressed his usual jealous behavior of growling and running after Maverick. (I have to say that my little fur-ball played good defense but it was quite annoying when you were just trying to play fetch with a tennis ball). As soon as Graham went after Maverick, my then-boyfriend grabbed him and tossed him in the pool. Now, before any of you animal lovers run to the phone and call Oprah or Ellen DeGeneres and shout animal cruelty, hear me out. The one thing that Grahamy feared was the water. Consequently, he associated the bad behavior with being put into the water, a situation that he did not like. From that day on, he began sitting on the sidelines to watch Maverick play ball instead of running deathly interceptions.

As soon as Graham did something that was wrong and inappropriate, he was disciplined. He learned that chasing and attacking Maverick was not right and he had to face the consequences for his actions. I was thrilled to have my first sense of control over him, and he became a better dog because of what happened. Ironically, after facing his fear of the water, he also came to understand and appreciate it. Soon Graham voluntarily put his paws into water, laid on the water's edge, and even endured a swimming lesson or two!

There have been times when I have done something wrong in my life and have felt disciplined by my loving Father. I have been thrown into water and have been made to swim my way out (as God watches every stroke I take to be sure that I do not drown). I am not suggesting that when something terrible happens to us, it is meant as a punishment from God. I am merely saying that if we are a Christian, if we know what is right and wrong and we choose to go against His will, God will allow us to be affected by our actions and behavior. He will gently guide us and show us what is right and wrong but ultimately, through free will, it is our choice whether we will change our behavior or not. Discipline is not a bad thing, it is done out of love. It teaches us moral values and it teaches children that it is not acceptable to hit, kick, and spit on elders or peers. I am not saying that children act perfectly when they are disciplined (my children specifically!), but they do develop a greater sense of respect, care, and obedience that undisciplined children do not experience. God wants us to respect, care, and obey Him and His commands. And, through doing that, we will gain understanding and appreciation for the life that He has given to us.

Side view Mirror: What is your experience with discipline? Think about how discipline has affected your life as a child and as an adult. Pray that you will be able to discern right from wrong and that God will protect you from making bad choices. And, thank Him for being a Father who disciplines.

Reflections on Interruptions

> "But the Lord provided a great fish to swallow Jonah, and Jonah was inside the fish three days and three nights." *Jonah 1:17*

One morning as I struggled to make sense of some things in my life, I was encouraged as I opened the following forwarded email:

"The only survivor of a shipwreck was washed up on a small, uninhabited island. He prayed feverishly for God to rescue him. Every day he scanned the horizon for help, but none seemed forthcoming. Exhausted, he eventually managed to build a little hut out of driftwood to protect him from the elements, and to store his few possessions. One day, after scavenging for food, he arrived home to find his little hut in flames, with smoke rolling up to the sky. He felt the worst had happened, and everything was lost. He was stunned with disbelief, grief and anger. He cried out, 'God! How could you do this to me?' Early the next day, he was awakened by the sound of a ship approaching the island! It had come to rescue him! 'How did you know I was here?' asked the weary man of his rescuers. 'We saw your smoke signal,' they replied.

The moral of the story: It's easy to get discouraged when things are going bad, but we shouldn't lose heart, because God is at work in our lives, even in the midst of our pain and suffering. Remember the next time your little hut seems to be burning to the ground. It just may be a smoke signal that summons the Grace of God."

It is so true. When bad things happen to us, the infamous first question is 'Why God, why?!' It doesn't always make sense why things don't go the way we would like them to go, or why we find ourselves at a dead end to a road we thought stretched out forever. There have been many times in my thirty plus years when I have found myself in a certain situation and thought I knew one hundred percent for sure what the best outcome would be for me, *and* everyone involved! Then all of a sudden my little hut would go up in flames and I was left trying to sort through all of the embers.

We can look at God's little interruptions as annoying, frustrating, confusing, or even maddening. Yet, it is a fact that we do not have the capability to see or know specific things that are going to happen in our future. Any psychic can debate this, but if this was the case, why didn't all of the psychics band together and stop those flights from going into the World Trade Centers on 9/11? If psychics claim to see the future, couldn't they sense and know that something bad was about to happen? I would think that if we knew what the future held, we would do anything we could to change certain things from happening. Thankfully God knows and sees the big picture and sometimes he puts up roadblocks in our path to protect, shield, and guide us into another direction. A direction that maybe we would never have given a second thought about.

In February of 2007, I was teaching children's fitness classes. I loved my job, the kids, my co-workers, and teaching. One weekend I experienced some hoarseness and I assumed that I just had a sore throat or I was coming down with a cold (which is funny to say living in Arizona). However, the weeks went by and it wasn't getting better. Then months went by and I had developed such hoarseness in my speaking that it began affecting my teaching and my position. I was broken and frustrated. My co-workers had to pick up my slack and I felt horrible and unenergetic. I finally made an appointment with an ENT and the doctor stated that due to overuse of my voice, I had developed swelling and calluses on my vocal chords. He suggested voice rest and medication and stated that if my voice was not better in a month, he would recommend surgery. This sounded crazy to me as I have always been naturally loud and had not experienced any voice problems in the past, even with teaching aerobics for over ten years. However, by this point, eight months had passed and I wanted my real voice back.

As many of my friends and family know, for me to be quiet is quite the oxymoron so it was challenging to go a whole month on voice rest. I received several hilarious jokes involving silence from my brother and was teased often by my friends. I was allowed to talk, but minimal, and I was not allowed to yell, throw my voice, whisper, or sing. It was difficult to take a month off of teaching but thankfully I had an understanding and supportive boss and was able to help out at work in other ways. During this month of 'rest' I began to question what I was supposed to be doing in life. I needed my voice if I wanted to continue to teach and without it, what would I do? Unexpectedly, I had to think of Plan B. And all I could think about was my creative side.

My long-term dream had been to use my creative talents and to grow my own creative business. Making cards, painting murals and scrapbooking had always been a side hobby of mine but I had always desired for it to be more. Thoughts of 'if only I had more time or money' usually stopped me from making any moves forward. I knew God had given me the creative talents but I knew I did not have any business-sense whatsoever, and I never seemed to find the extra time or money needed to get a small business off the ground and running. But there I was, without a voice and a possible upcoming job loss if I didn't find my voice again. I thought about looking for other jobs but knew if I found something else, I would still be putting my dreams on hold. Or, I could just take a leap of faith and trust God in knowing there was a reason for this absurd voice loss situation.

The month went by and I found myself sitting in the ENT office again. After putting the scope through my nose and down my throat to determine my prognosis, the doctor said, to his surprise, that my voice had healed up nicely and he would not have to schedule a procedure. I was in shock that I had managed to get out of yet another surgery!

If I had not experienced that ongoing hoarseness, I would never have thought about a change in my job or career path. I would never have been quiet enough to listen to God and find my rest and peace in Him. He not only made my direction clear during that month, he also healed my voice after I sought Him and realized that a leap of faith was just what the Ultimate Doctor and Healer ordered. Everything seemed to fall into place after that (which is always a good sign to me that God has something to do with it!). I would not say that it was always easy after I resigned from my job but somehow, someway God provided. My business did not start bringing in record sales or hitting a million dollar mark but if God had not interrupted me, I may not have been open to following my dreams. Sometimes he has to allow an interruption in order for us to see what He has for us. And, it is usually something bigger and better than we could ever imagine.

I love the little hut story because it reminds me, once again, that there really is a reason for everything that happens. God can turn a bad situation into something very good. It is evident to me that when we find ourselves shipwrecked, God does have a way of getting us through it and getting through to us. We might not like how he chooses to teach or save us, but I must admit that I have thanked God many times for setting my huts on fire.

Side view Mirror: Is your 'hut' on fire? Are you feeling hopeless? Take time to pray and evaluate your situation. Pray for guidance and a clearing through the fog. And, thank Him for saving you when everything else is in flames.

Reflections on Self-Esteem

"I praise you because I am fearfully and wonderfully made; your works are wonderful, I know that full well." *Psalm 139:14*

One of the very first memories that I can recall was when I was about four years old. The year was 1981 and I was sitting with my grandma in a hospital waiting room. I wasn't sure what we were waiting for; the only thing that I remember was that I wanted to watch Sesame Street. There was someone else in the room with us and my grandma asked them if it was okay if she could change the channel to accommodate my request. I have no idea how long I was watching my favorite show when my dad showed up in the doorway with a funny blue cap on. It was a split door and when my grandma picked me up to look over the door I saw what we were waiting for. I was told that it was my baby brother. I wasn't really sure what that meant; but I soon found out that he was staying with us, for good. He was like a doll of mine, except this one made a lot of noise and needed mom and dad's attention quite often. But, it was okay because I was a proud big sister.

When I was a toddler I didn't question my existence or my life purpose. I didn't feel the need to value myself against the latest fashions or the best hairstyle. Life was carefree and full of free-range play and catching fireflies at dark. I didn't compare myself to other toddlers and quite frankly, I was unaware of anyone around me if there was a coloring book and a new set of crayons in front of me. But, all that changed when grade school began.

All of a sudden I was keenly aware of who I was. I was scared to death to raise my hand in class and I never had the coolest thing for show-in-tell time. I was quiet and shy and all the other kids were outgoing and playful. I was shorter than everyone else in class and not as pretty as the other girls. Even a bus driver ridiculed me because of how little I was. I was humiliated, and the first thoughts of not being good enough took root.

Growing up I didn't really understand what was going on between my parents but I knew the tension was high and that my Mom was not happy. She would often show signs of depression by shutting down emotionally and keeping to herself, which made the lines of communication rather difficult. One day I walked into her room and her shades were drawn. It was dark but I made my way over to her bed and asked if she was okay. She didn't turn towards me but through tears I heard her say that she didn't want to live anymore. I remember a sinking feeling in my stomach as I walked away. As a young and impressionable tween I thought, "*If my Mom doesn't want to be around, I must not be good enough.*"

When I found out that my ex-husband did in fact have an affair it was another strike against my confidence and self-esteem. When we took our vows I vowed to be his one and only and knowing that he had been with someone else intimately rocked my world, and not in a good way. I didn't fathom that I would have to compete with another woman in my marriage and that I would hear my husband say that he loved someone else. Feelings of inadequacy overwhelmed my thoughts and I kept hearing, "You're still not good enough. You will never be good enough."

I don't share these instances to place blame on anyone or to claim victim status. I share these to show that in all of these situations I was placing my value on other people's words and actions. And, unfortunately, I was giving Satan a foothold into my thoughts. He loves whispering and taunting us with his web of lies. He loves consuming us with thoughts of failure, inadequacy and ridicule.

After college I was a case manager in the mental health field for about seven years. I remember in one of my first trainings that our language was important. Instead of making a statement that I worked with a mentally ill person, it was better to say, "person with a mental illness". This is out of respect and the value is then placed on the person rather than the disability. It changes the perspective on things and this is what I had to do in my own life. I had to change the way that I was thinking and who I was listening to. This cycle would be continuing in my life today had I not intentionally made the choice to truly believe God's word and his promises. Often people wonder if they are hearing God or not. You can know without a shadow of a doubt if it is God or not if what you hear matches up to His word. Inward healing cultivates outward healing.

I would not be good for anyone else if I didn't first find my value and esteem in God. People are going to disappoint us, face it, that's life! God created the garden as a perfect place for us and due to humanity falling into temptation the world is no longer how God originally designed it. But God gives us hope. If we allow Him to speak into our lives we can discern the truth from the lies. Negativity is an emotional cancer and positive affirmations soothe the soul.

One of my all-time favorite children's books is *You Are Special* by Max Lucado. This story is a beautiful and clever tale of how much God loves us and is an amazing reminder that He uniquely CREATED us. It's about how some people in this world only care about outward appearances and make us feel that we are not special or good enough, but our loving creator KNOWS us and He did NOT make a mistake when He brought us into existence. In His presence we are whole and we can be confident in His love and pursuit for us. The illustrations in the book are so genuine and precious and I still tear up every time I read it to my children.

So, who am I? I am still a proud big sister. I am still a person that is vertically challenged who hears short-jokes on a regular basis. But, I am also a child of God and I am His daughter. I am saved by the grace of God and I am His little girl. I am smart, confident, pretty and talented because He made me that way. I am special, worthy, and blessed immensely. I am FABULOUS! Get to know yourself the way God sees you. Do not let others, or circumstances, define who you are. Do not give the devil a foothold into your thinking. Do not allow the devil to twist the truth and do not believe that you are not good enough. You are wanted, you are loved, and you are HIS.

Don't get me wrong, this is much easier said than done. There are still days where I question my talent and times when I don't feel pretty. But I can now recognize these thoughts and know that they are not ones that are building me up. I can visualize myself at God's feet and can hear Him telling me that I am good enough. And, that's good enough for me.

Side view Mirror: How do you define yourself? Our society overemphasizes outward beauty over inward beauty and many times one's self-esteem can get wrapped up in what others think instead of what God thinks. Pray that He will help you find your worth in Him. Be in His word and listen to His affirmations over your life. And, thank Him for His overwhelming love and for numbering all of the hairs on your head.

Reflections on Love

*"Love one another. As I have loved you, so you must love one another." **John 13:34***

I have been in love, and I have fallen out of love. I have been smitten, in awe, and impressed by a man, and I have been hurt, disappointed, and broken by the same species. So, what's the point? Why fall in love? Why should we even bother putting the time and effort into someone? Why go through all the pain? Why should we open our hearts up time and time again only to leave ourselves vulnerable and risk another possible heartache? On the other hand, why not?

Love was never meant to be an easy task at all times. I think that is why the greatest commandment God gives us is to love one another. However, in our human nature, we all have different ways, responses, and preferences on how we do that. It has been proven through science, and in personal experiences, that men and women are not only from different planets, they can be from different galaxies as well. At times it can seem like an impossible task in trying to find 'The One' from a particular galaxy, yet alone the same planet.

The usual process of finding such love is a fun event typically called dating. And, I have to admit I experienced my fair share of dates, including a long list of blind dates and set-ups. As soon as I announced my divorce was official it was as if everyone I knew had someone absolutely perfect just waiting for me, along with their own personal opinions as to how my new love story should play out. I looked at dating as a way of meeting new people and tried not to get my hopes up too high. In each scenario, I would open the door to a new face, a new personality, and a new possibility. And, in most cases, it turned out to be just dinner at a new place to eat.

It is hard not to look back and chuckle at the experiences though, and to give some of them names. There was the "Old Guy" with two daughters and a blatant revengeful heart against his ex-wife, "Muscle-Man" who, in the process of bulking his body up, had shrunken his own head and was a couple fries short of a Happy Meal, "Mr. Commitment" who gave me love coupons on the second date, "Dr. Dan" the dud, "Military Man" who had 'Pride and Arrogance' etched on his forehead, and "Shark-Face" the guy who was a little too aggressive and practically ate my face off when he tried to kiss me, just to name a few. None of these gentlemen were bad, just not for me. Would I ever find him? At times I wondered if I had missed something. Was I on the right path? Would I get a second chance at marriage?

I have come to learn that love stories are like snowflakes. Each one is beautiful but no two are alike. If I were to interview all of my friends and family as to how they fell in love with their significant other, each one would have something different to tell. There are stories of childhood sweethearts that were set up in the wombs of their parents and spending the rest of their life together was inevitable. There are stories of people who saw their love from a distance and just knew they were meant to be together. There are stories of couples who didn't even like each other when they first met and in time, a love like no other grew between them. There are stories about couples who met and were married within three weeks, and stories of couples that took a little longer to become 'one'. However no matter how one's love story is told, love is always worth the risk.

As Erica Jong quoted, "Love is everything it's cracked up to be. That's why people are so cynical about it. It really is worth fighting for, risking everything for. And the trouble is, if you don't risk everything, you risk even more." It had been very easy for me to be cynical and to vent about the fact that my love story may not have illuminated itself in the timing that I had hoped it would. We all have been through things that have hurt us or circumstances that may have built our walls of defense up a little higher. Yet our wall of defense does not have to be built by stacking blocks one on top of the other, they can be built as stepping stones. Taking something from every experience and bettering ourselves as we climb up the stairs.

I have had my heart broken on several occasions and at times I was left confused and saddened. However, looking back on my single, dating, and love experiences, I truly believe I would not be who I am today or where I am in my life had those circumstances unfolded any other way. In all actuality, I would have missed out on some amazing and life-changing experiences. There were times when I needed to be single in order to get my focus back on track, there were times I dated for mere socialization and an occasional confidence-boost, and there were times when I dated and fell in love with someone and from that relationship, learned more about myself, love, and my relationship with God. None of these experiences were a loss. Yes, I risked a broken heart, but if I had not risked, I may not be in a position to see things in a different light and from a different perspective. I would not have grown and healed in ways I didn't know I needed or opened my eyes up to someone again who may not be perfect, but is perfect for me.

Side view Mirror: Have you ever been in love? God calls us first to love Him with all of our heart, soul, and mind and then commands us to love one another. Reflect on your priorities and seek Him first. Pray that He will show you things that you may need to work on and pray for openness and humility. And, thank Him for granting the desires of your heart, even if they don't unfold like you would have had planned.

Reflections on Second Chances

*"The Lord blessed the latter part of Job's life more than the former part." **Job 42: 12***

I started babysitting when I was eleven. I always enjoyed being around kids and thought for sure that I would be a young mom. But, in my mid-twenties, when all of my other friends were announcing their first pregnancies, I was announcing my divorce. I attended baby shower after baby shower and put on my best smile through the 'wrap-the-mom-to-be's-tummy-in-toliet-paper-to-see-how-big-she-is' game. I was truly happy for my friends but it was hard knowing that my dream of becoming a mom was on hold. And, I had no idea how long that hold would be.

As I have shared in all of my stories, God used my divorce to cultivate many experiences, revelations, and realizations in my life. I found healing, hope and strength in ways that I could never have imagined. He brought me to a place where

I found a deeper relationship with Him and experienced true forgiveness. And, after all of the tears, trials and testimonies, He did give me a second chance at marriage.

Jeremy and I were married in the cutest little white chapel that I had ever seen in the backwoods of Missouri. It was a beautiful day complete with an intimate gathering of our closest family and friends. The cake was delicious, the first dance was priceless and the whole day was memorable.

Have you ever heard that old saying, "If you want to make God laugh, tell Him your plans"? Well, there had been many times over the course of my life that I had not talked to God about my life, but rather I talked at God about what I wanted Him to do in my life. I never gave him the ample opportunity to respond back. I always left the conversation where I hung up the phone and left Him hanging. I often told God in many of my closed conversations that I wanted to experience pregnancy and have several children. I didn't hear it then, but there is no doubt that He was saying, "Oh daughter, just wait for what I have planned."

It turns out that God decided that we should become parents two months after we got married. I do know that pregnancy is typically a nine-month process but in our case, it didn't happen that way. In fact, when our first child came, he was eighteen months old, fast on his feet and had a small vocabulary. Welcome to parenthood!

To make a long story a bit shorter, Jeremy's nephew, Nate, had been placed in the foster care system due to parental neglect and drug abuse issues. Jeremy and I petitioned the

State soon after we were married and we were granted temporary placement for Nate. We had no idea what we were in for but it didn't take long to find out that we had quite the stubborn and strong-willed little man on our hands. He had emotional issues, such as detachment and fits of rage, and I often worried that a neighbor would call the police when Nate would go into one of his extreme tantrums. We missed hearing our pastor's full sermons for about a year because we kept getting called out to the nursery due to Nate's biting habits. There were nights where sweat would be dripping from my body because I had held him in a pretzel hold for so long just so he wouldn't hurt himself. There were many times when I questioned God as to what I was supposed to do and how I was supposed to handle Nate, but over and over I would sense that God was affirming to me that He had prepared me for this. Every situation I had endured-my divorce, my jobs, my faith, and my experiences had led me to Nate.

We fought for Nate for eighteen months before the court granted permanent placement and allowed us to adopt him. It was one of the happiest days of my life when the judge signed those papers and announced that we were his official parents! I was the mother of a three year old and I felt a keen sense of awareness that my past had paved the way to this one particular moment.

Several months after we adopted Nate, I was watching my husband and Nate play. I sensed God telling me that our family was not yet complete and by that time next year we would have another child. My hopes were high as I assumed that meant that we would win the battle of infertility and become pregnant. But, months kept passing and my hopes dwindled. I began to doubt that I had even heard from God.

Four months went by and out of the blue I received a phone call from my Mom telling me that one of her friend's teenage daughters was pregnant. She wanted to give the baby up for adoption and our names had come up in a conversation. In a series of events that can only be explained as God-ordained (and has so many amazing details that it could be a book in itself!) we were chosen to adopt this baby.

Less than a year from the day that I had sensed God whispering to me, our family was complete with a sweet baby boy who we named Alexander. He is truly a gift from God and I still find myself in awe of the whole situation. We have remained super close to his birth mom and both her and her family have become a natural extension of our own. In fact, I later found out in conversation that Xander had been conceived around the same time I felt the Holy Spirit speaking to me.

There are times in our life when we go through situations that we cannot see all of the pieces fit together. There are certainly many times in my own life that I think that God has taken too long of a coffee break and I demand that He get back to work. Yes, I had once dreamed of experiencing pregnancy and being a young mom but now I cannot imagine my family coming together in any other way. God knows what He is doing and I have to think that there is a good reason for our infertility. Some pregnancies do not go as smooth and maybe

He has, unknowing to me, shielded me from something traumatic happening to my life, or a baby's life.

I am also grateful that I am an older parent now and that I have these personal experiences tucked inside my apron of motherhood. I don't always know the answers to the questions that I have on this earth but I do know that God placed these specific children in our lives. My children are my own children even though I did not birth them. They are my sweet baby boys who I am privileged and honored to learn from everyday. Our hearts have been forever changed through the gift of adoption and it is a joy to feel firsthand what God must feel when He adopts us into His forever family. I feel immensely blessed to be chosen by God to be Jeremy's wife and the mother to Nate and Xander. I am humbled and so grateful to God for second chances.

Side View Mirror: Have you prayed for a second chance in an area of your life? Maybe in a relationship, in a job opportunity, or in a friendship? Just like in the book of Jonah, God is the God of second chances. We may have to sit in a whale for awhile until we can learn some things but God has a way of throwing us out, no matter how dirty and damaged we are, and set our feet in the right direction.

Reflections on Eternity

> "I am the Alpha and the Omega, the Beginning and the End. To the thirsty I will give water without cost from the spring of the water of life." ***Revelation 21:6***

Have you ever had a friend recommend a 'good' movie to you? They say, "This movie was so good, you will love it!" only to watch it and think, "What was my friend thinking? That was horrible!" Everyone's opinions are different, which ultimately, make this world go around. Some people think that sushi is REALLY good (me included), while others get nauseous just THINKING about eating raw food. Some people think that sci-fi movies are awesome, while others (me included) think otherwise. And, some people think that "good" people go to heaven and "bad" people go to hell. So if this is the case, then who defines who is "good" and "bad"? Hopefully not the friend that just recommended that movie to you!

The fact of the matter is, God defines "good" and "bad", however, those are not the prerequisites when getting into heaven. Unfortunately, the world sugarcoats our eternal destination. Every funeral that I have ever attended made indication that the person was "in a better place" even if the person was a proclaimed aetheist. The truth of the matter is… if you do not believe in God and have him in your heart, you will not go to heaven when we die. This is not meant as a judgmental statement because it is not my opinion or idea. It is made by the truth that is found in the Bible. God does not count up our "good" deeds and our "bad" deeds to determine if we will enter through those pearly gates. You don't get to slide in with a certain number of marks. That's just not how it works.

To the world we can be the greatest and most giving person ever, but still not get into heaven if Jesus is not Lord of our life. And, on the contrary, we can be looked at as horrible in the world's eyes and yet make it to heaven if we ask forgiveness, repent (turn away from) our sins, and ask Jesus into our heart. There is a reason why Jesus went to the cross. It wasn't because He wanted to, it's because He knew he HAD to endure the cross so that we may live. FOREVER. He loves us THAT much.

Let's unwrap just a few of the myths out there:

Myth #1: "I believe that there is a God so I will go to heaven." Truth: In James 2:19 it says, "You believe that there is one God. Good! Even the demons believe that-and shudder." In other words, the demons believe and KNOW that there is a God but yet they are not in heaven with Jesus. God wants us to KNOW Him, not just know OF Him.

Myth #2: "Everyone goes to heaven when they die." Truth: It is clearly written in scripture that this is not the case. In John 14:6 it says, "I am the way and the truth and the life. No one comes to the Father except through me." And, in Matthew 7:13 it says, "Enter through the narrow gate. For wide is the gate and broad is the road that leads to destruction, and many enter through it. But small is the gate and narrow the road that leads to life, and only few find it." In this passage the "destruction" mentioned is hell and the "life" is heaven.

Myth #3: "I just need to be good, do good, and live a good life." Truth: In Matthew 10:32-33, 38-39 it says, "Whoever acknowledges me before men, I will also acknowledge him before my Father in heaven. But whoever disowns me before men, I will disown him before my Father in heaven. Anyone who does not take up his cross and follow me is not worthy of me. Whoever finds life will lose it, and whoever loses his life for my sake will find it." Also in Ephesians 2:8 it says, "For it is by grace you have been saved, through faith-and this is not from yourselves, it is the gift of God-not by works so that no one can boast." We are all born with sin, therefore none of us are perfect. So, we can attempt to do as many good works as we want, but unless we understand what He did for us on the cross and acknowledge that God is God and we are not, then living a "good" life just isn't going to cut it. We must accept Jesus into our heart otherwise we will truly lose our life when we die. But, the glory of the story is that death does NOT have to be OUR end.

I asked our senior pastor, Clint Sprague, why God even gave us free will. Why didn't he just create all of us to love him? I mean, come on, He's GOD! He can do anything! Why bother to put the tree in the garden and the sin card into the equation? My pastor simply stated, "Because God didn't create us to be robots." He didn't want us to love Him out of obligation, he wanted us to love him out of devotion. He didn't want to *force* us, He wanted us to *desire* a relationship with Him. By giving us the choice, it is our decision and is a matter of our HEART. We cannot look to anyone else to make this choice for us and we are the only ones who can live this out. We have to make the effort and the sacrifice. True love happens when we have a choice NOT to love.

Mortality is certainly not a fun subject, especially when it comes up in conversation with young children at a funeral. So, I don't want to come off as morbid here, but I will be honest and say that my husband and I have already started talking about these myths and truths with our children. They have already heard, through my husband and I and other fellow believers, that Christ died for our sins. They have already heard that there is a heaven and a hell and not everyone goes to heaven. And, they have already heard that you need to have Jesus in your heart if you want to spend eternity with Him. However, even in speaking these truths, unfortunately, I cannot save my children or make the decision to follow Christ for them. And, I also cannot force my beliefs or the gift of salvation onto anyone else either. We all have to grasp it and we have to WANT a personal relationship with Jesus Christ. God DID give us free will. All of us. It is OUR choice as to what our eternal destiny is going to be. And, I don't know about you, but I certainly don't want to live just a "good" life, die, and THEN find out.

Side View Mirror: Do you have a personal relationship with Jesus Christ? Does your heart belong to Him? Nothing in this world is secure except for the hope that we have in Jesus. If you have never accepted Jesus into your heart and would like to, ask Him now. You can be in relationship with GOD. The one true GOD. The living GOD who created us and who loves us wholeheartedly. You don't have to be good enough to come to Him, He accepts you just as you are.

A Note From The Author

Dear Readers,

I feel incredibly blessed to have this personal project published, and I just wanted to thank you so much for taking the time to read it. I thank God for this opportunity to share some of my experiences, revelations and faith with you.

Most of these chapters were written prior to my children, and oh, how my stories have grown since they have come into my life! My husband thinks I should collaborate them and call it, "Burps, Farts and Butt Jokes-My Life with Boys", but that title is still up for discussion!

No matter what you are facing, know that God created you, He loves you and He will meet you where you are. I pray you will be blessed, find hope in Him, and encouragement through others. And, may you always remember that God knows exactly what we need, even when we are so sure of what we want. Hand over the wheel and enjoy the ride friends!

Blessings,
Stephanie Dulin
Numbers 6:24-26